IN CELEBRATION
OF WOMEN

Great Quotations Publishing Company
Glendale Heights, Illinois

0 43422 69511 9

Compiled by Peggy Schaffer

— • —

© 1993 Great Quotations Publishing Company

Published in the United Stated by

Great Quotations Publishing Company,
1967 Quincy Court
Glendale Heights, Illinois 60139

Printed in Hong Kong
ISBN: 1-56245-072-7

W here women are,
the better things are
implied if not spoken.

— Amos Bronson Alcott

Women love the lie that saves their pride,
but never an unflattering truth.

— Gertrude Atherton

Here's to woman!
That we could fall into her arms
without falling into her hands.

— Ambrose Bierce

I believe a woman's place
is not only in the home,
but in the House and Senate
and throughout the government.

— Lyndon Johnson

I want to make a policy statement.
I am unabashedly in favor of women.

— Lyndon Johnson

To conclude that women are unfit
to the task of our historic society
seems to me the equivalent
of closing male eyes to female facts.

— Lyndon Johnson

Women may be a whole oceans deeper
than we are,
but they are also a whole paradise better.
She may have got us out of Eden,
but as a compensation
she makes the earth very pleasant.

— John Oliver Hobbes

——————————————————

The most precious possession
that ever comes to a man in this world
is a woman's heart.

— Josiah G. Holland

——————————————————

I would rather live with the woman I love
in a world full of trouble,
than to live in heaven
with nobody but men.

— Robert Ingersoll

There is in every woman's heart
a spark of heavenly fire,
which lies dormant
in the broad daylight of prosperity;
but which kindles up,
and beams and blazes
in the dark hour of adversity.

— Washington Irving

When you educate a man,
you educate an individual;
when you educate a woman,
you educate a whole family.

— Dr. Charles McIver

——————————————————————

Opportunities are usually disguised
by hard work,
so most people don't recognize them.

— Ann Landers

——————————————————————

Once made equal to man,
woman becomes his superior.

— Socrates

The best cosmetic in the world
is an active mind
that is always finding something new.

— Mary Meek Atkeson

Life was meant to be lived,
and curiosity must be kept alive.
One must never, for whatever reason,
turn his back on life.

— Eleanor Roosevelt

I believe in hard work.
It keeps the wrinkles out of the mind
and the spirit.
It helps to keep a woman young.

— Helena Rubenstein

As soon as you feel too old to do a thing,
do it!

— Margaret Deland

When you get into a tight place
and it seems you can't go on,
hold on,
for that's just the place and the time
that the tide will turn.

— Harriet Beecher Stowe

It is not easy to find happiness in ourselves,
and impossible to find it elsewhere.

— Agnes Repplier

Indecision is fatal.
It is better to make a wrong decision
than build up a habit of indecision.

— Marie Beynon Ray

We ought to be able
to learn some things second hand.
There is not enough time for us
to make all the mistakes ourselves.

— Harriet Hall

You can take no credit for beauty at 16.
But if you are beautiful at 60,
it will be your own soul's doing.

— Marie Stopes

The test of a man
is how well he is able
to feel about what he thinks.
The test of a woman
is how well she is able to think
about what she feels.

— Mary S. McDowell

No one can make you feel inferior
without your consent.

— Eleanor Roosevelt

Optimism is the faith
that leads to achievement.
Nothing can be done
without hope and confidence.

— Helen Keller

Nothing in life is to be feared.
It is only to be understood.

— Marie Curie

I have started school.
A young woman beside me
asked what I wanted to be.
I said that I would like to become
more of what I am already.
She said she wished she had my ego.
I told her it took time.

— Ethel Seldin-Schwartz

There is a woman at the beginning
of all great things.

— De Lamartine

Men have sight; women insight.

— Victor Hugo

No one knows like a woman
how to say things which are at once
gentle and deep.

— W. Aikman

The intuitions of women
are better and readier
than those of men;
her quick decisions
(without conscious reasons)
are frequently far superior
to a man's most careful deductions.

— W. Aikman

A woman's guess
is much more accurate
than a man's certainty.

— Rudyard Kipling

Next to God,
we are indebted to women;
first for life itself,
and then for making it worth having.

— Bovee

I think somehow,
we learn who we really are
and then live with that decision.

— Eleanor Roosevelt

And the trouble is,
if you don't risk anything,
you risk even more.

— Erica Jong

Life begets life.
Energy creates energy.
It is by spending oneself
that one becomes rich.

— Sarah Bernhardt

One is not born a woman,
one becomes one.

— Simone De Beauvoir

Why not seize the pleasure at once?
How often is happiness destroyed
by preparation,
foolish preparation!

— Jane Austen

Trouble is a part of your life,
and if you don't share it,
you don't give the person who loves you
enough chance to love you enough.

— Dinah Shore

Courage is the price
that life exacts for granting peace.

— Amelia Earhart

You can't be brave
if you've only had wonderful things
happen to you.

— Mary Tyler Moore

To live is so startling
it leaves little time for anything else.

— Emily Dickinson

I like living.
I have sometimes been wildly,
despairingly, acutely miserable,
racked with sorrow,
but through it all
I still know quite certainly
that just to be alive is a grand thing.

— Agatha Christie

I f you have made mistakes...
there is always another chance for you...
you may have a fresh start
any moment you choose,
for this thing we call "failure"
is not the falling down,
but the staying down.

— Mary Pickford

Reality is something you rise above.

— Liza Minelli

Mistakes are part of the dues
one pays for a full life.

— Sophia Loren

Progress in civilization
has been accompanied by
progress in cookery.

— Fannie Farmer

...that is the best —
to laugh with someone
because you both think
the same things are funny.

— Gloria Vanderbilt

One of the things about equality
is not just that you be treated
equally to a man,
but that you treat yourself
equally to the way you treat a man.

— Marlo Thomas

It is hard to fight an enemy
who has outposts in your head.

— Sally Kempton

She did observe,
with some dismay, that,
far from conquering all,
love lazily sidestepped
practical problems.

— Jean Stafford

It is easy to be independent
when you've got money.
But to be independent
when you haven't got a thing —
that's the Lord's test.

— Mahalia Jackson

Always there remain portions of our heart
into which no one is able to enter,
invite them as we may.

— Mary Dixon Thayer

I always felt that the great high privilege,
relief and comfort of friendship
was that one had to explain nothing.

— Katherine Mansfield

Tact is after all a kind of mindreading.

— Sarah Orne Jewett

Fond as we are of our loved ones,
there comes at times during their absence
an unexplained peace.

— Anne Shaw

"Stay" is a charming word
in a friend's vocabulary.

— Louisa May Alcott

Superior people never make very long visits.

— Marianne Moore

You may be disappointed if you fail,
but you are doomed if you don't try.

— Beverly Sills

Light tomorrow with today!

— Elizabeth Barrett Browning

We can do no great things —
only small things with great love.

— Mother Theresa

In youth we learn;
in age we understand.

— Marie Ebner-Eschenbach

The beauty of the world,
which is so soon to perish,
has two edges, one of laughter,
one of anguish,
cutting the heart asunder.

— Virginia Woolf

There's a time when you have to explain
to your children
why they're born,
and it's a marvelous thing
if you know the reason by then.

— Hazel Scott

One never notices what has been done;
one can only see what remains to be done.

— Marie Curie

Creative minds have always been known
to survive any kind of bad training.

— Anna Freud

To be successful,
the first thing to do is fall in love
with your work.

— Sister Mary Lauretta

Think wrongly,
if you please,
but in all cases
think for yourself.

— Doris Lessing

I am never afraid of what I know.

— Anna Sewell

I'll not listen to reason.
Reason always means
what someone else has got to say.

— Elizabeth Cleghorn Gaskell

Women are repeatedly accused
of taking things personally.
I cannot see any other honest way
of taking them.

— Marya Mannes

We don't see things as *they* are,
we see them as *we* are.

— Anais Nin

Age is something that doesn't matter,
unless you are a cheese.

— Billie Burke

D on't compromise yourself.
You are all you've got.

— Betty Ford

When choosing between two evils,
I always like to try
the one I've never tried before.

— Mae West

One wonders what would happen
in a society in which there were
no rules to break.
Doubtless everyone would quickly die
of boredom.

— Susan Howatch

In passing, also, I would like to say
that the first time Adam had a chance
he laid blame on woman.

— Nancy Astor

If only we'd stop trying to be happy,
we could have a pretty good time.

— Edith Wharton

Adventure is something you seek
for pleasure, or even for profit,
like a gold rush or invading a country;
...but experience is what really happens to you
in the long run;
the truth finally overtakes you.

— Katherine Anne Porter

We all live in suspense,
from day to day,
from hour to hour;
in other words,
we are the hero of our own story.

— Mary McCarthy

Ｉf you obey all the rules
you miss all the fun.

— Katherine Hepburn

It's the good girls who keep the diaries;
the bad girls never have the time.

— Tallulah Bankhead

The real art of conversation
is not only to say the right thing
in the right place
but to leave unsaid the wrong thing
at the tempting moment.

— Dorothy Nevill

To be meek, patient, tactful,
modest, honorable, brave,
is not to be either manly or womanly;
it is to be humane.

— Jane Harrison

Unfortunately, sometimes people
don't hear you
until you scream.

— Stefanie Powers

A man has to be Joe McCarthy
to be called ruthless.
All a woman has to do
is put you on hold.

— Marlo Thomas

The trouble with being in the rat race
is that even if you win,
you are still a rat.

— Lily Tomlin

When a man gets up to speak,
people listen, then look.
When a woman gets up,
people look;
then, if they like what they see,
they listen.

— Pauline Frederick

If only one could tell true love
from false love
as one can tell mushrooms
from toadstools.

— Katherine Hepburn

When you have a baby,
you set off an explosion in your marriage,
and when the dust settles,
your marriage is different from what it was.
Not better, necessarily;
not worse, necessarily;
but different.

— Nora Ephron

The average man is more interested
in a woman who is interested in him
than he is in a woman with beautiful legs.

— Marlene Dietrich

A woman without a man
is like a fish without a bicycle.

— Gloria Steinem

We don't believe in rheumatism
and true love
until after the first attack.

— Marie Von Ebner-Eschenbach

Whenever you want to marry someone,
go have lunch with his ex-wife.

— Shelley Winters

The one important thing
I have learned over the years
is the difference between
taking one's work seriously
and taking one's self seriously.
The first is imperative
and the second is disastrous.

— Margot Fonteyn

It is the friends that you can call up
at 4 a.m. that matter.

— Marlene Dietrich

Personally, I think if a woman
hasn't met the right man
by the time she's 24,
she may be lucky.

— Deborah Kerr

Do not, on a rainy day,
ask you child
what he feels like doing,
because I assure you
that what he feels like doing,
you *won't* feel like watching.

— Fran Lebowitz

Sometimes I wonder if men and women
really suit each other.
Perhaps they should live next door
and just visit now and then.

— Katherine Hepburn

Absence does not make
the heart grow fonder,
but it sure heats up the blood.

— Elizabeth Ashley

Show me a woman
who doesn't feel guilty
and I'll show you a man.

— Erica Jong

Whenever I dwell for any length of time
on my own shortcomings,
they gradually begin to seem mild,
harmless, rather engaging little things,
not at all like the staring defects
in other people's characters.

— Margaret Halsey

I don't sit around thinking
that I'd like to have another husband;
only another man
would make me think that way.

— Lauren Bacall

Woman's discontent increases
in exact proportion to her development.

— Elizabeth Stanton

While others may argue
about whether the world ends with a bang
or a whimper,
I just want to make sure
mine doesn't end with a whine.

— Barbara Gordon

When he is late for dinner
and I know he must be either having an affair
or lying dead in the street,
I always hope he is dead.

— Judith Viorst

It's never too late —
in fiction or in life —
to revise.

— Nancy Thayer

I think the one lesson I have learned
is that there is no substitute
for paying attention.

— Diane Sawyer

I'd like to grow very old
as slowly as possible.

Age does not protect you from love.
But love, to some extent,
protects you from age.

— Jeanne Moreau

The thing women have got to learn
is that nobody gives you power.
You just take it.

— Roseanne Barr Arnold

Man forgives woman anything
save the wit to outwit him.

Kids learn more from example
than anything you say.
I'm convinced they learn very early
not to hear anything you say,
but watch what you do.

— Jane Pauley

True strength is delicate.
— Louise Nevelson

Were women meant to do everything —
work *and* have babies?

— Candice Bergen

If I am too strong for some people,
that's their problem.

— Glenda Jackson

It is better to die on your feet
than to live on your knees.

— Dolores Ibarruri

It is sad to grow old
but nice to ripen.

— Brigitte Bardot

Luck is a matter of preparation
meeting opportunity.

— Oprah Winfrey

The only interesting answers
are those that destroy the questions.

— Susan Sontag

Men are taught to apologize
for their weaknesses,
women for their strengths.

— Lois Wyse

You grow up the day you have your first real laugh at yourself.

— Ethel Barrymore

The phrase "working mother" is redundant.

— Jane Sellman

When you're in love,
you put up with things that,
when you're out of love,
you hate.

— Miss Manners

The way I see it,
if you want the rainbow,
you gotta put up with the rain.

— Dolly Parton

Marrying a man is like buying something
you've been admiring for a long time
in a shop window.
You may love it when you get it home,
but it doesn't always go
with everything else.

— Jean Kerr

I don't believe man
is a woman's natural enemy.
Perhaps his lawyer is.

— Shana Alexander

From birth to age 17
a girl needs good parents.
From 18 to 35 she needs good looks.
From 36 to 55 she needs a good personality.
From 56 on she needs good cash.

— Sophie Tucker

...perhaps one has to be very old
before one learns how to be amused
rather than shocked.

— Pearl S. Buck

My true friends have always given me
that supreme proof of devotion,
a spontaneous aversion
for the man I loved.

— Colette

Ideally, couples need three lives;
one for him,
one for her,
and one for them together.

— Jacqueline Bisset

How many cares one loses
when one decides
not to be something,
but to be someone.

— Coco Chanel

The ultimate lesson all of us have to learn
is unconditional love,
which includes not only others
but ourselves as well.

— Elisabeth Kubler-Ross

Love is a fire.
But whether it is going to
warm your hearth
or burn down your house,
you can never tell.

— Joan Crawford

If love is the answer,
could you please rephrase the question?

— Lily Tomlin

Being powerful is like being a lady.
If you have to tell people you are,
you aren't.

— Margaret Thatcher

Every great mistake has a halfway moment,
a split second when it can be recalled
and perhaps remedied.

— Pearl S. Buck

Women of the world,
united without any regard
for national or racial divisions,
can become a most powerful force
for international peace.

— Coretta Scott King

Good health is more
than just exercise and diet.
It is really a point of view
and a mental attitude.
You can have the strongest body,
but it's not good
unless the person inside of you
has strength and optimism.

— Angela Lansbury

The characteristics
that they criticize you for —
that you are strong-minded,
that you make firm and tough decisions —
are also characteristics which,
if you were a man,
they would praise you for.

— Margaret Thatcher

Motherhood and homemaking
are honorable choices for any woman,
provided it is the woman herself
who makes those decisions.

— Molly Yard

If a man doesn't want a woman
to express her own opinions and be funny,
then he's not worth impressing.

— Carol Burnett

A woman's place in society
is wherever her talents, energies,
and determination will carry her.

— L. Douglas Wilder

...what a gift —
to give life, to bear a child!
Strength comes from that.
Emotionally and spiritually,
women may be able to lift the world.

— Bruce Smith

To love what you do and feel
that it matters —
how could anything be more fun?

— Katherine Graham

Men, their rights and nothing more;
Women, their rights and nothing less.

— Susan B. Anthony

We fought hard.
We gave it our best.
We did what was right.
And we made a difference.

— Geraldine Ferraro

It is worse than folly...
not to recognize the truth,
for in it lies the tinder for tomorrow.

— Pearl S. Buck

Those who do not know how to weep
with their whole heart
don't know how to laugh either.

— Golda Meir

I've had an exciting life;
I married for love
and got a little money along with it.

— Rose Kennedy

I don't know anything about luck.
I've never banked on it,
and I'm afraid of people who do.
Luck to me is something else;
hard work and realizing
what is opportunity and what isn't.

— Lucille Ball

To be successful,
a woman has to be better at her job
than a man.

— Golda Meir

Old age is like a plane
flying through a storm.
Once you are aboard,
there's nothing you can do.

— Golda Meir

The important thing in acting
is to be able to laugh and cry.
If I have to cry,
I think of my sex life.
If I have to laugh,
I think of my sex life.

— Glenda Jackson

You don't seem to realize
that a poor person who is unhappy
is in a better position
than a rich person who is unhappy.
Because the poor person has hope,
he thinks money would help.

— Jean Kerr

Some people are more turned on by money
than they are by love...
In one respect they're alike.
They're both wonderful
as long as they last.

— Abigail Van Buren

Ninety-eight percent of the adults
in this country
are decent, hard-working, honest Americans.
It's the other lousy two percent
that get all the publicity.
But then we elected them.

— Lily Tomlin

I keep the telephone of my mind
open to peace, harmony, health,
love and abundance.
Then whenever doubt, anxiety, or fear
try to call me,
they keep getting a busy signal
and soon they'll forget my number.

— Edith Armstrong

Whether women are better than men
I cannot say —
but I can say they are certainly no worse.

— Golda Meir

...love is the only thing
that we can carry with us when we go,
and it makes the end so easy.

— Louisa May Alcott

The future belongs
to those who believe in the beauty
of their dreams.

— Eleanor Roosevelt

This became a credo of mine...
attempt the impossible
in order to improve your work.

— Bette Davis

Self-expression must pass into communication
for its fulfillment.

— Pearl S. Buck

A happy woman
is one who has no cares at all;
a cheerful woman
is one who has cares
but doesn't let them get her down.

— Beverly Sills

Success can make you go one of two ways.
It can make you a prima donna,
or it can smooth the edges,
take away the insecurities,
let the nice things come out.

— Barbara Walters

OTHER TITLES BY GREAT QUOTATIONS PUBLISHING COMPANY

199 Useful Things to Do With A Politician
201 Best Things Ever Said
A Lifetime of Love
A Light Heart Lives Long
A Teacher Is Better Than Two Books
As A Cat Thinketh
Cheatnotes On Life
Chicken Soup
Dear Mr. President
Father Knows Best
Food For Thought
Golden Years, Golden Words
Happiness Walks On Busy Feet
Heal The World
Hooked on Golf
Hollywords

In Celebration of Women
Life's Simple Pleasures
For Mother - A Bouquet of Sentiment
Motivation Magic
Mrs. Webster's Dictionary
I'm Not Over The Hill ...
Reflections
Romantic Rendezvous
Sports Page
So Many Ways To Say Thank You
The ABC's of Parenting
The Best Of Friends
The Birthday Astrologer
The Little Book of Spiritual Wisdom
Things You'll Learn, If You Live Long Enough

GREAT QUOTATIONS PUBLISHING CO.

1967 Quincy Court
Glendale Heights, IL 60139-2045
Phone (708) 582-2800
FAX (708) 582-2813